Bassoon

Name____

MW01486986

Foundations for Superior Performance
Warm-Ups and Technique for Band
by Richard Williams and Jeff King

A comprehensive and sequential book of warm-ups, scales, technical patterns, chord studies, tuning exercises, and chorales for concert band.

Designed to organize the daily rehearsal and advance the performance level of the ensemble.

Practical and efficient exercises in all twelve major keys developed in the classroom.

Table of Contents

ISBN 0-8497-7006-8

Kjos Neil A. Kjos Music Company • *Publisher*

W32BN

Concert F Around The Band

Each instrument will play concert F in their middle register. The bassoon is a concert pitched instrument, there is no transposition for the bassoon.

Copy the note in measure one into measure two.

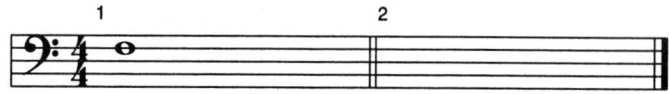

Your director will divide the band into various sections or groups for the listening drill Concert F Around The Band.

Once the instruments have been placed into groups, write the name of the instrument(s) in the appropriate box below (every box may not be used).

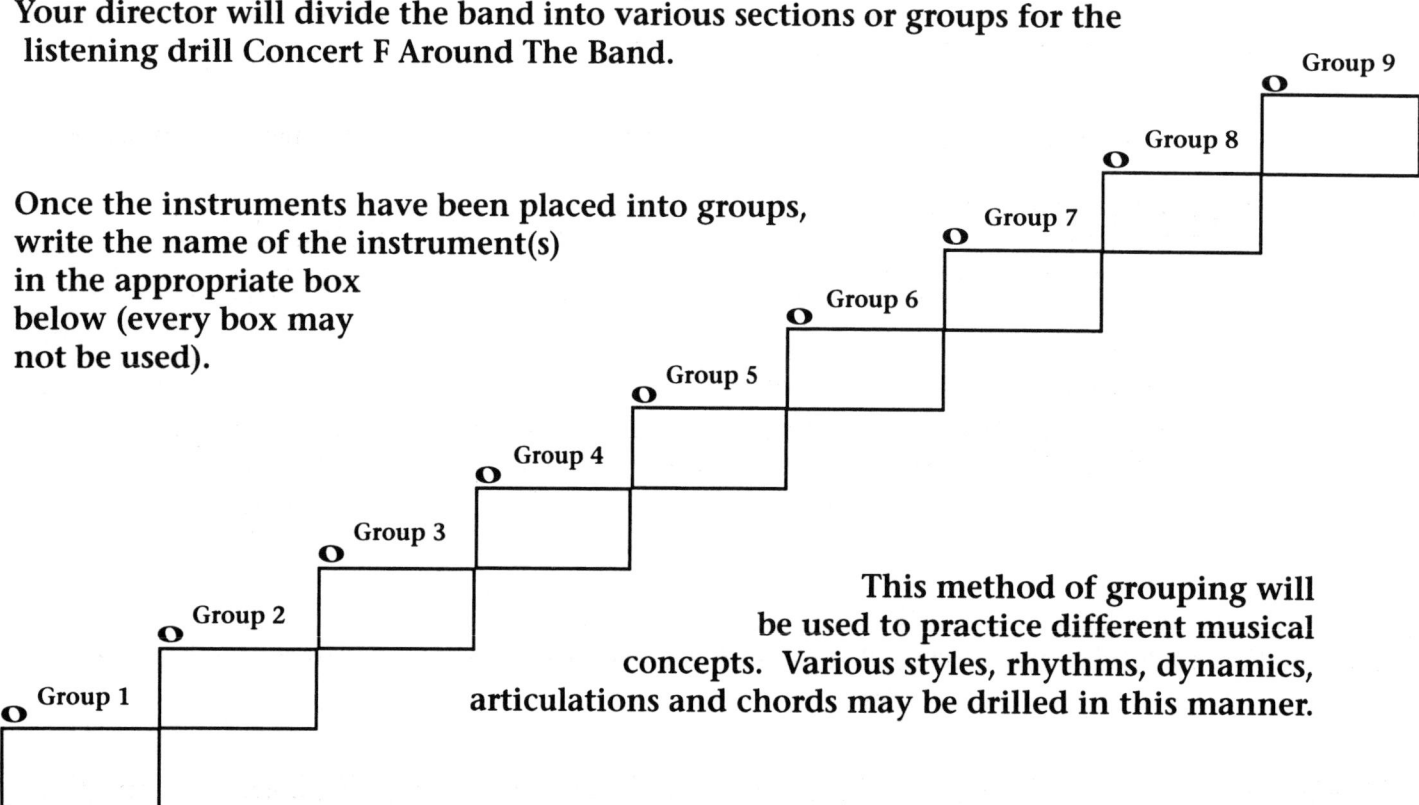

This method of grouping will be used to practice different musical concepts. Various styles, rhythms, dynamics, articulations and chords may be drilled in this manner.

As you play the exercise, keep the following concepts in mind:

• hand off each note without creating "holes" between the attacks

• work for a smooth "block" shape to each note (no bumps in the sound)

• match the primary parts of each note (attack-sustain-release)

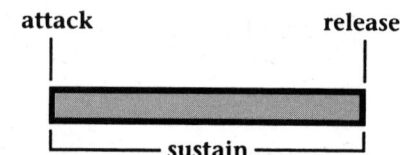

• match intonation, intensity, volume, tone quality, and the "body of sound"

• be aware of the different colors (timbres) of the instrument groups and their location in the room

• listen from the bottom groups and balance low-middle-high

Articulation Exercises

Articulations: A Study in Styles

Four connected quarter-notes (tenuto). The sound of one note "touches" the next note.

Four quarter-notes in "lifted" style. The attack is the same as tenuto, but the end of the note is tapered.

Four quarter-notes "lifted and short" (staccato). Separated and detached (half full value).

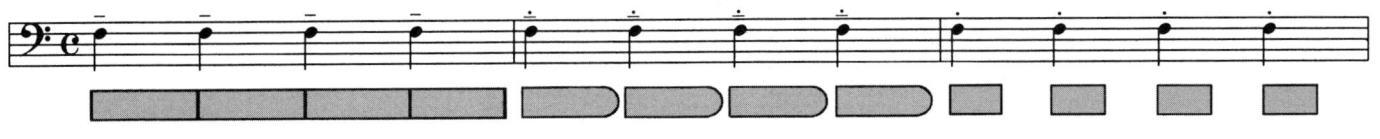

Eighth-notes in connected style.

Eighth-notes in lifted and short style.

Eighth-note triplets in connected style.

Eighth-note triplets in a detached style (bounced).

Sixteenth-notes in a connected style.

Articulation Exercise on Concert F

Long Tones

Concert F Descending

1

2

Long Tone 1

1a

1b

1c

1d

Long Tone 2

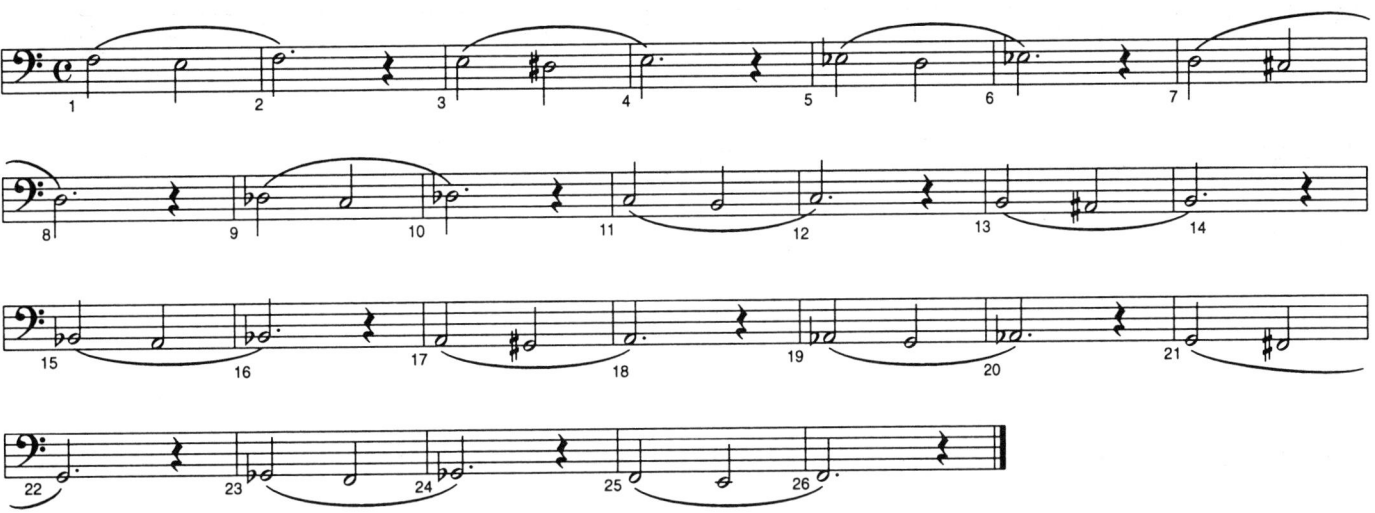

Long Tone 3

3a   *intervals of a minor 2nd*   *intervals of a major 2nd*

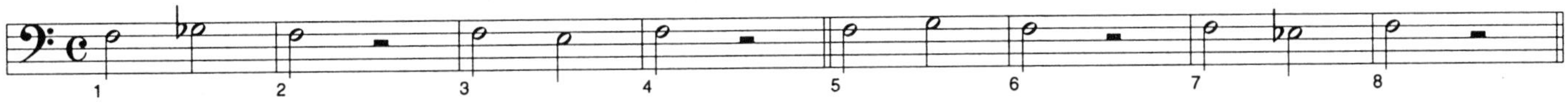

intervals of a minor 3rd   *intervals of a major 3rd*

intervals of a perfect 4th   *intervals of an augmented 4th*

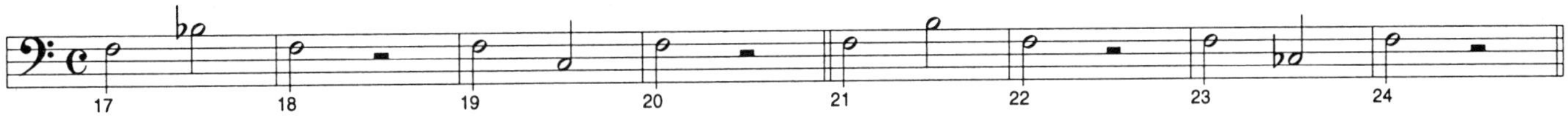

intervals of a perfect 5th

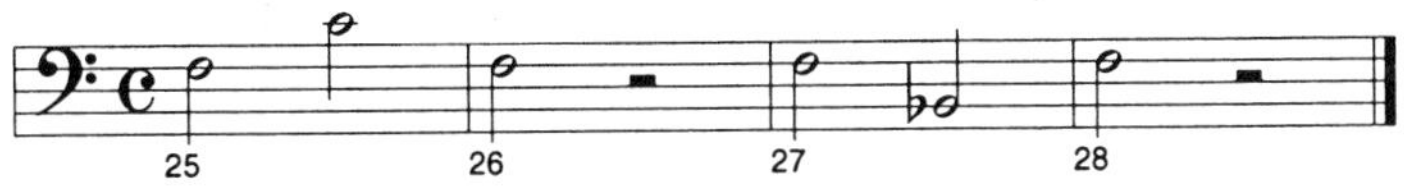

3b   *intervals of a minor 2nd*   *intervals of a major 2nd*   *intervals of a minor 3rd*

intervals of a major 3rd   *intervals of a perfect 4th*   *intervals of an augmented 4th*

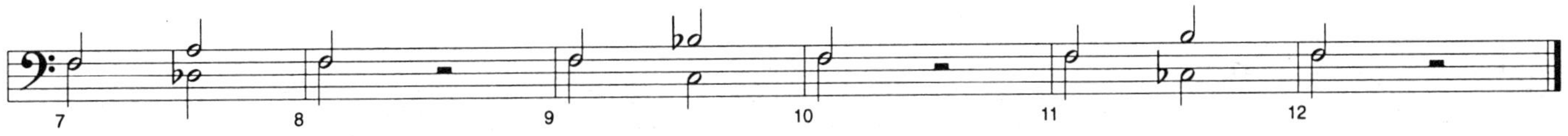

Warm-Up Set 1

Option 1 (unison "lip slur" with brass)

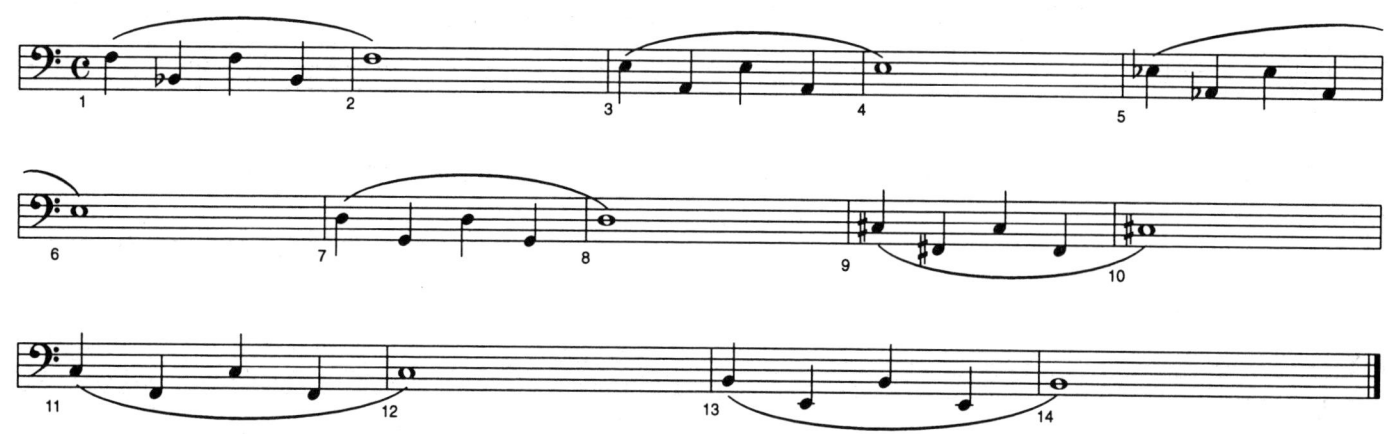

Option 2 (octave slur study with brass lip slur)

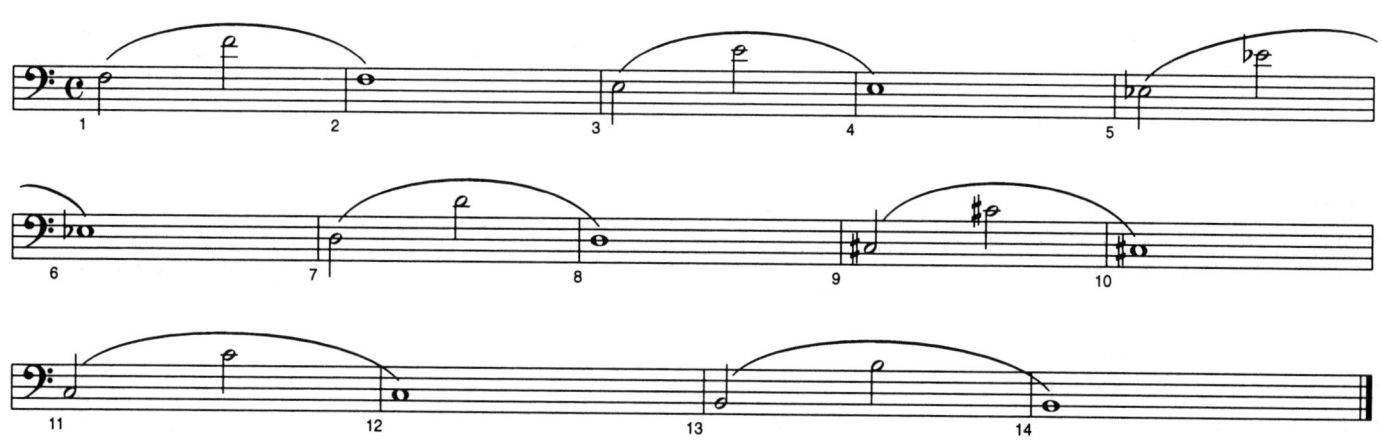

Options 3, 4, & 5 (technical patterns with brass lip slurs)

Warm-Up Set 2

Option 1 (unison "lip slur" with brass)

Option 2 (octave slur study with brass lip slur)

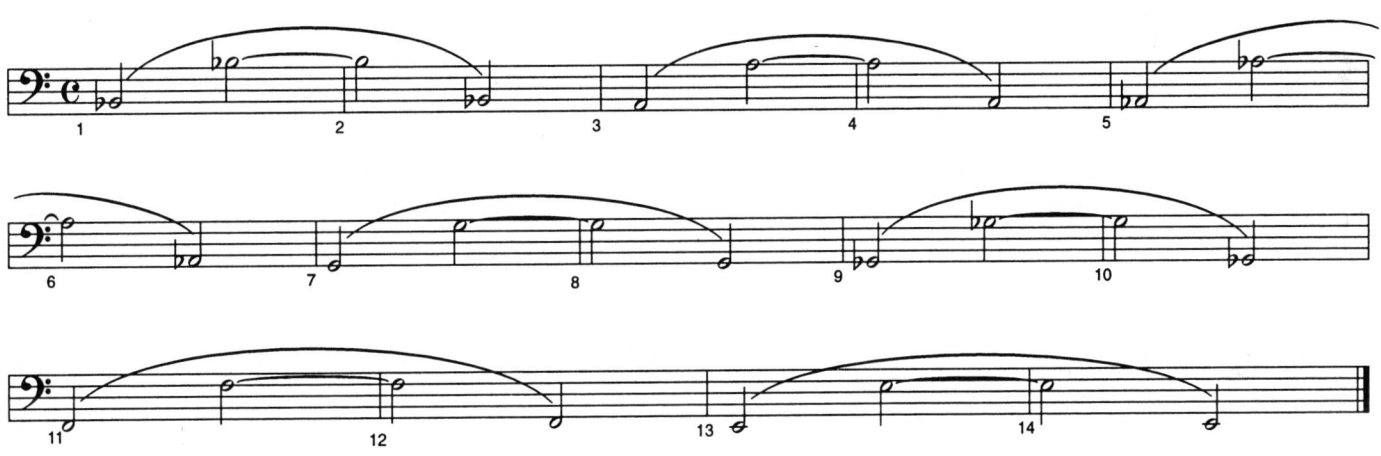

Options 3, 4, & 5 (technical patterns with brass lip slurs)

Articulation Patterns:

Warm-Up Set 3

Option 1 (unison "lip slur" with brass)

Option 2 (octave slur study with brass lip slur)

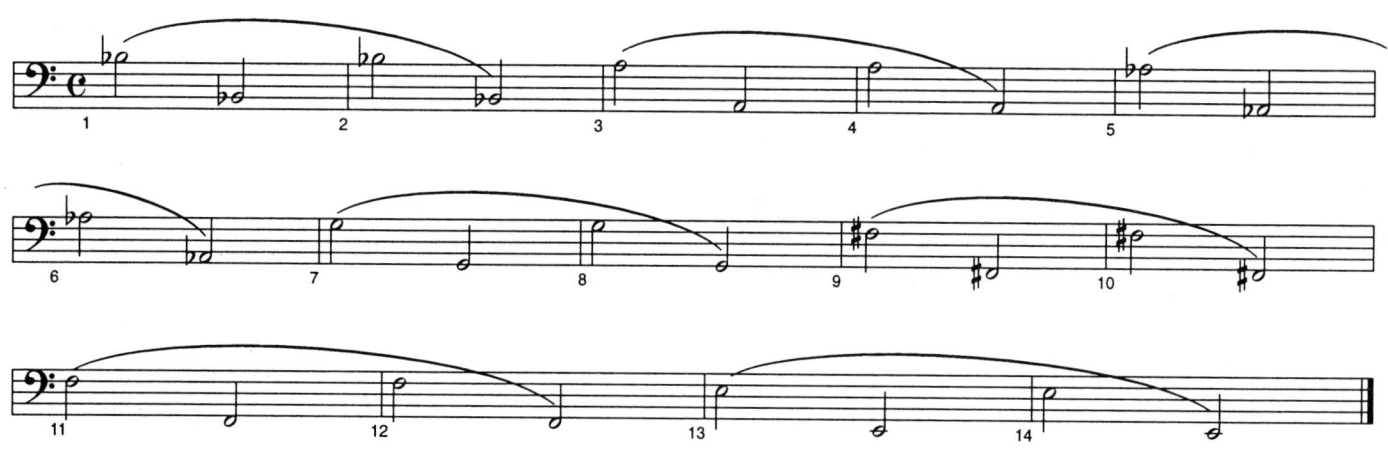

Options 3, 4, & 5 (technical patterns with brass lip slurs)

Warm-Up Set 4

Option 1 (unison "lip slur" with brass)

Option 2 (octave slur study with brass lip slur)

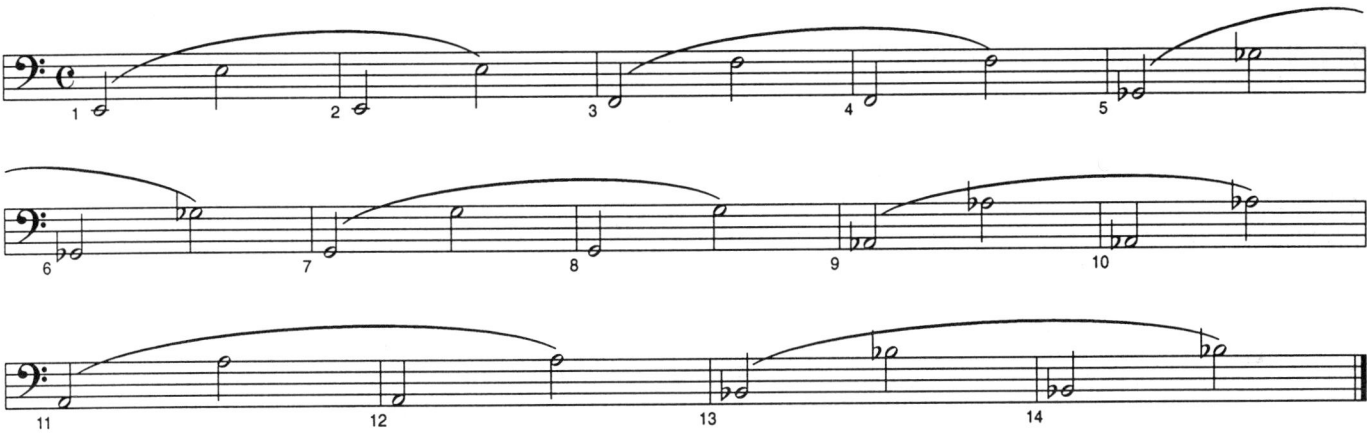

Options 3, 4, & 5 (technical patterns with brass lip slurs)

Technical Exercises in the Key of B♭

Major Scale

Natural Minor

Harmonic Minor

Melodic Minor

Mini-Scale & Tonic Arpeggio

(also practice 8vb)

Scale Pattern *articulations:*

Scale Pattern 2*

Scale in Thirds*

(also practice 8va)

Interval Study

Triads of the B♭ Scale

I ii iii IV V vi vii°

Chord Study 1*

Chord Study 2 - *articulations:*

Technical Exercises in the Key of F

Major Scale

Natural Minor

Harmonic Minor

Melodic Minor

Mini-Scale & Tonic Arpeggio

(also practice 8va w/cue note)

Scale Pattern 1 *articulations:*

Scale Pattern 2*

Scale in Thirds*

Interval Study

Triads of the F Scale

Chord Study 1*

Chord Study 2 - *articulations:*

Technical Exercises in the Key of C

Major Scale

Natural Minor

Harmonic Minor

Melodic Minor

Mini-Scale & Tonic Arpeggio

(also practice 8va)

Scale Pattern 1 *articulations:

(also practice 8vb)

Scale Pattern 2*

(also practice 8vb)

Scale in Thirds*

Interval Study

Triads of the C Scale

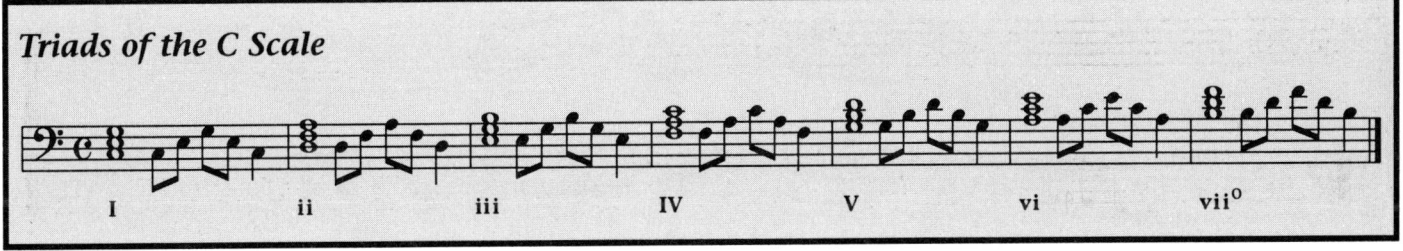

I   ii   iii   IV   V   vi   vii°

Chord Study 1*

Chord Study 2 - *articulations:*

Technical Exercises in the Key of G

Major Scale

Natural Minor

Harmonic Minor

Melodic Minor

Mini-Scale & Tonic Arpeggio

Scale Pattern 1 *articulations:

Scale Pattern 2*

Scale in Thirds*

Interval Study

Triads of the G Scale

Chord Study 1*

Chord Study 2 - *articulations:*

Technical Exercises in the Key of D

Major Scale

Natural Minor

Harmonic Minor

Melodic Minor

Mini-Scale & Tonic Arpeggio

(also practice 8va w/cue note)

Scale in Thirds - articulations:

Technical Exercises in the Key of A

Major Scale

Natural Minor

Harmonic Minor

Melodic Minor

Mini-Scale & Tonic Arpeggio

Scale in Thirds - articulations:

Technical Exercises in the Key of E

Major Scale

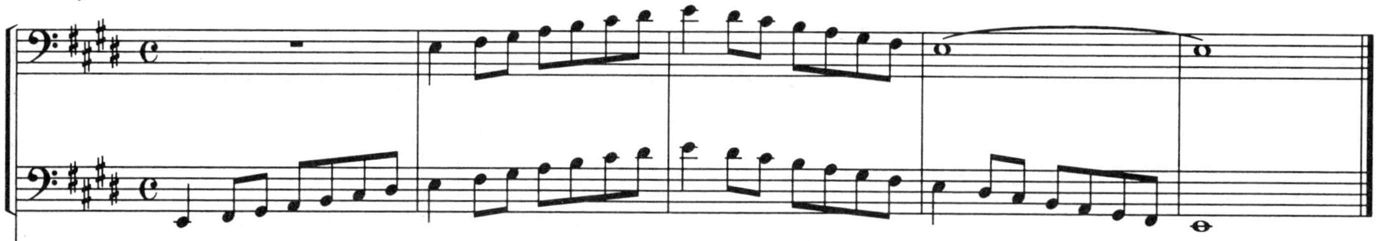

Natural Minor

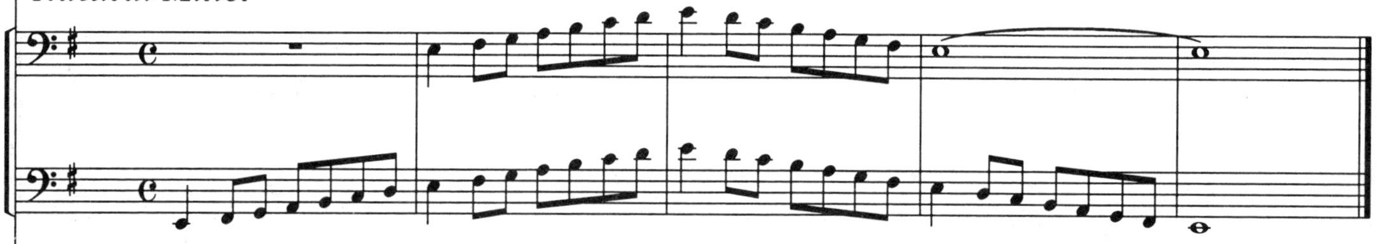

Harmonic Minor

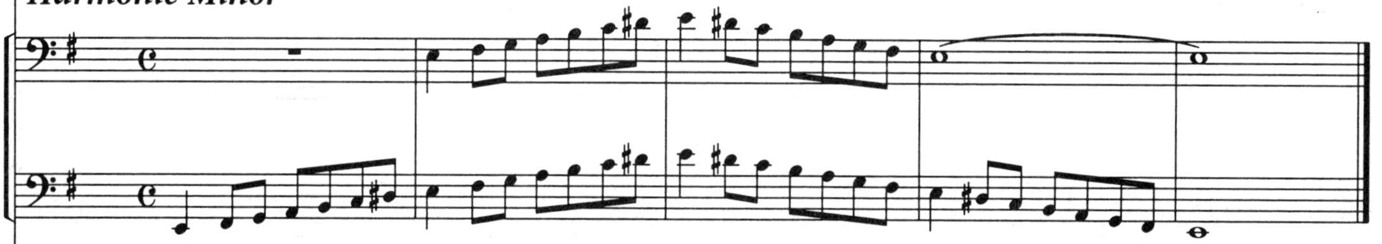

Melodic Minor

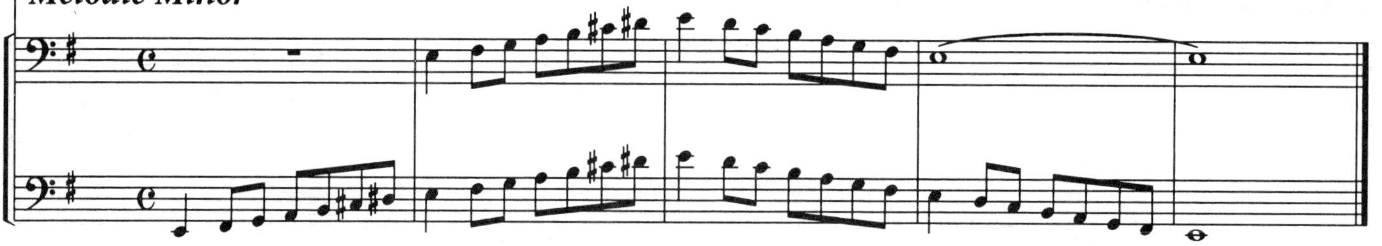

Mini-Scale & Tonic Arpeggio

(also practice 8va w/cue note)

Scale in Thirds - articulations:

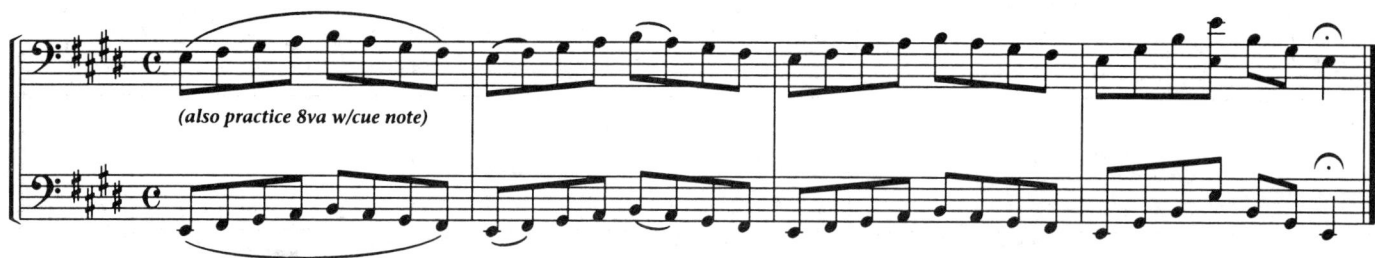

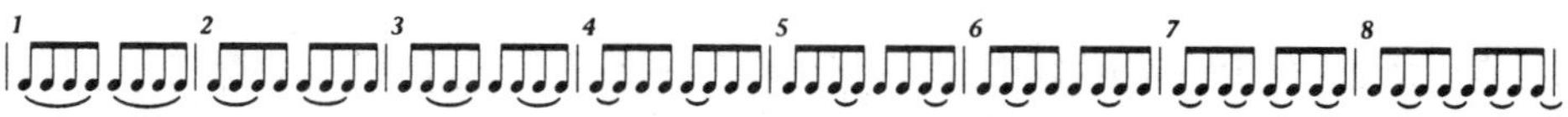
1
2
3
4
5
6
7
8

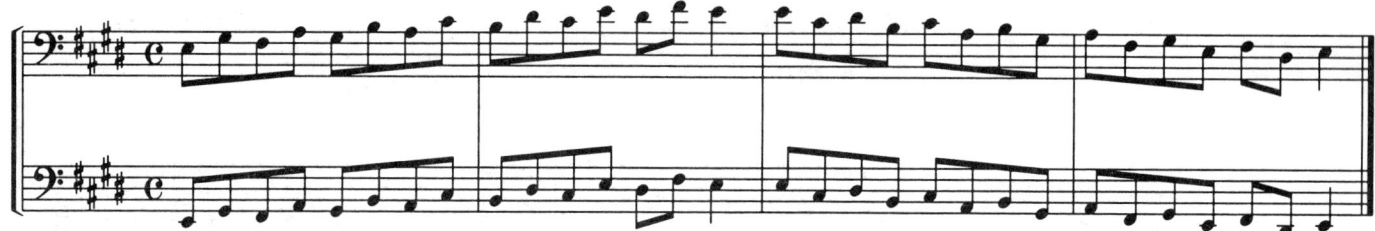

Technical Exercises in the Key of B

Major Scale

Natural Minor

Harmonic Minor

Melodic Minor

Mini-Scale & Tonic Arpeggio

(also practice 8vb)

Scale in Thirds - *articulations:*

Technical Exercises in the Key of G♭

Major Scale

Natural Minor

Harmonic Minor

Melodic Minor

Mini-Scale & Tonic Arpeggio

Scale Pattern 1 *articulations:

Scale Pattern 2*

Scale in Thirds*

Interval Study

Triads of the G♭ Scale

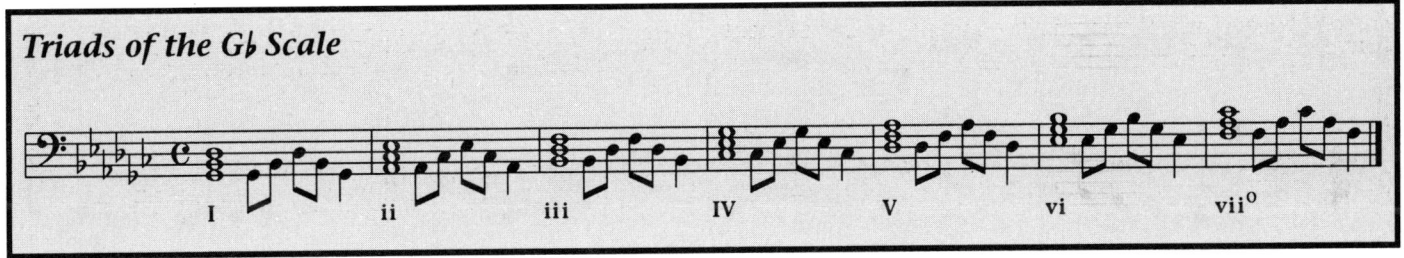

I   ii   iii   IV   V   vi   vii°

Chord Study 1*

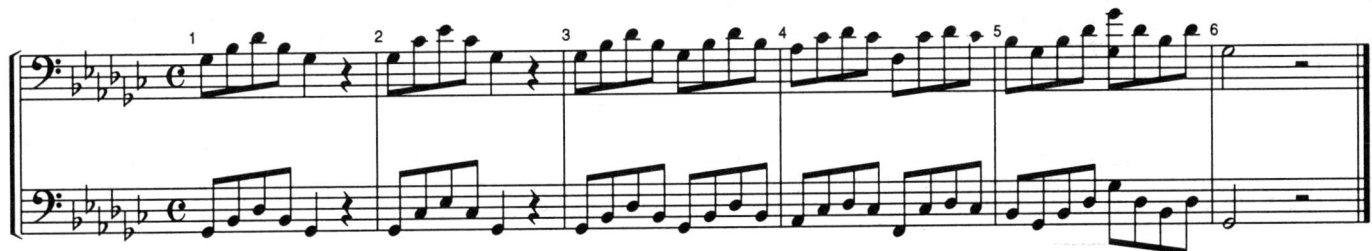

Chord Study 2 - articulations:

Technical Exercises in the Key of D♭

Major Scale

Natural Minor

Harmonic Minor

Melodic Minor

Mini-Scale & Tonic Arpeggio

(also practice 8va w/cue note)

Scale Pattern 1 **articulations:*

(also practice 8va)

Scale Pattern 2*

(also practice 8va)

Scale in Thirds*

Interval Study

Triads of the Db Scale

I   ii   iii   IV   V   vi   vii°

Chord Study 1*

Chord Study 2 - articulations:

Technical Exercises in the Key of A♭

Major Scale

Natural Minor

Harmonic Minor

Melodic Minor

Mini-Scale & Tonic Arpeggio

Scale Pattern 1 *articulations:*

Scale Pattern 2*

Scale in Thirds*

Interval Study

Triads of the A♭ Scale

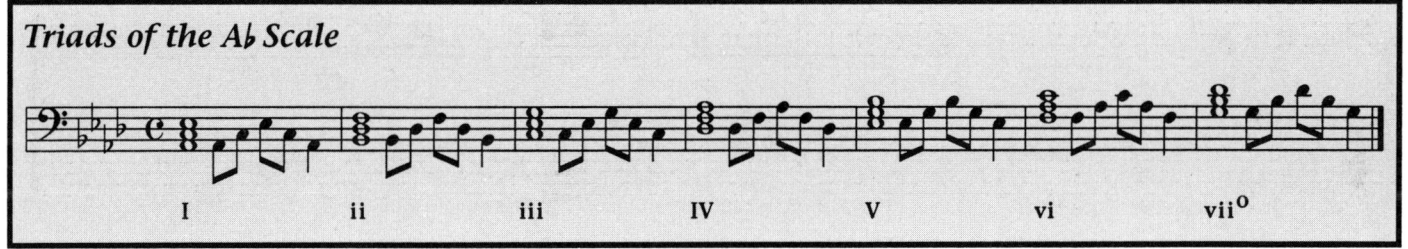

I   ii   iii   IV   V   vi   vii°

Chord Study 1*

Chord Study 2 - articulations:

Technical Exercises in the Key of E♭

Major Scale

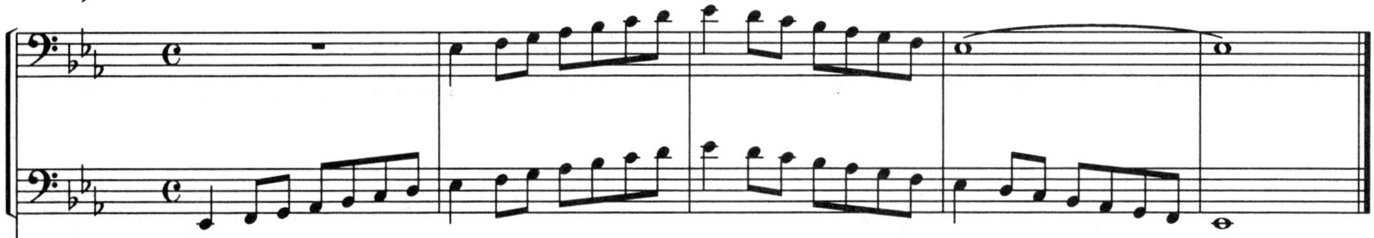

Natural Minor

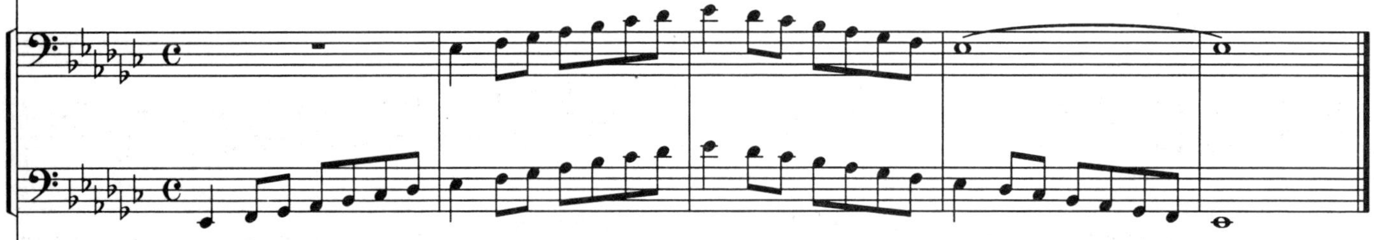

Harmonic Minor

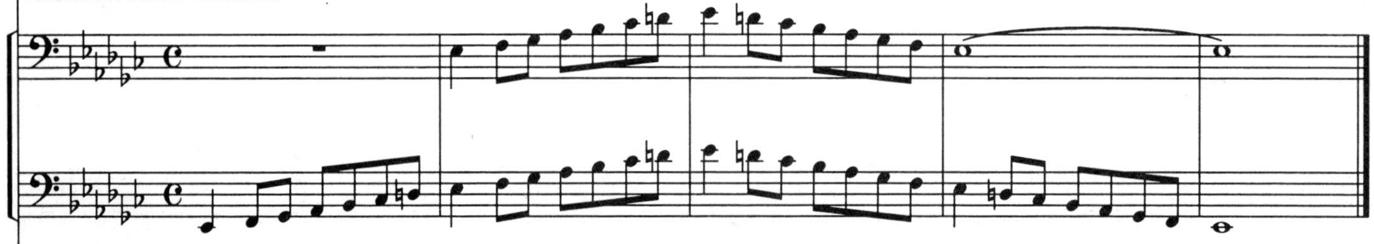

Melodic Minor

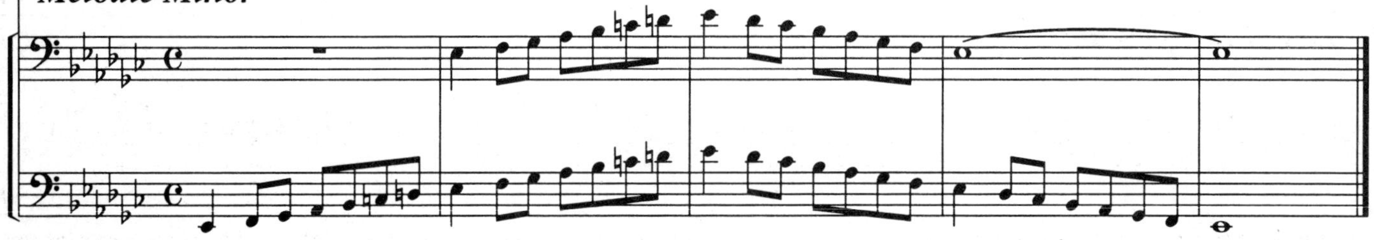

Mini-Scale & Tonic Arpeggio

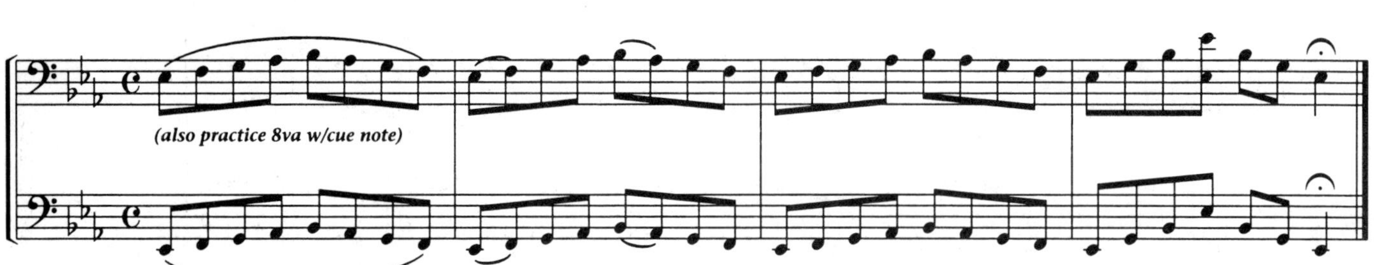
(also practice 8va w/cue note)

Scale Pattern 1 *articulations:

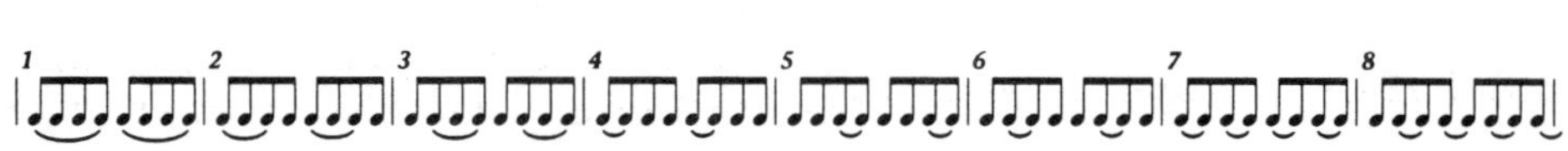
1
2
3
4
5
6
7
8

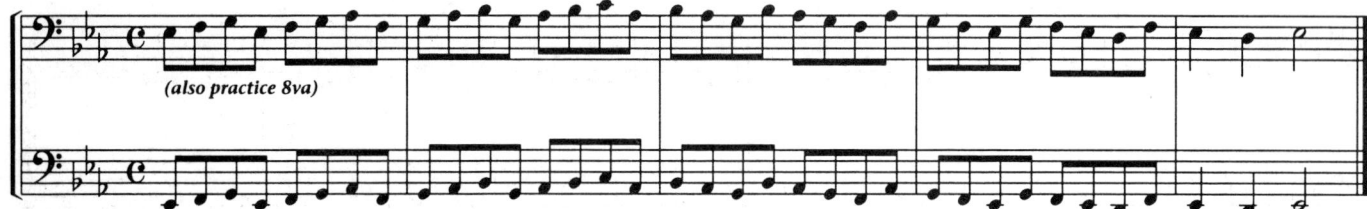

(also practice 8va)

Scale Pattern 2*

(also practice 8va)

Scale in Thirds*

Interval Study

Triads of the E♭ Scale

I   ii   iii   IV   V   vi   vii°

Chord Study 1*

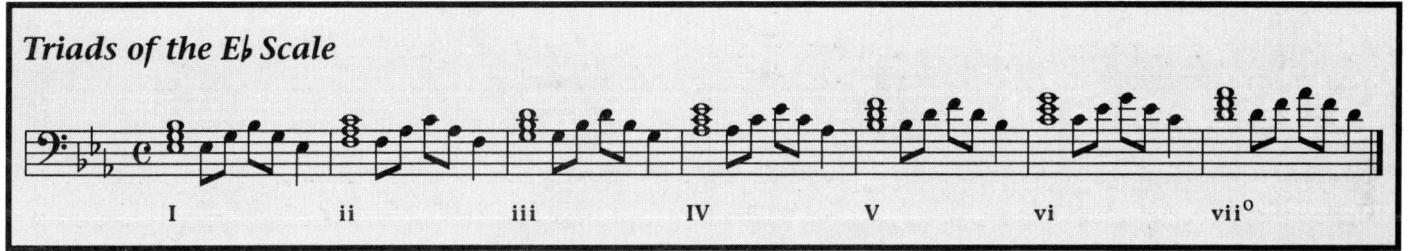

Chord Study 2 - articulations:

Chorales & Tuning Exercises in B♭

Interval Tuning

1 Intervals from tonic (major 3rd, perfect 4th, perfect 5th)

2 Intervals of a major 3rd on the I-IV-V-I chord progression

3 Intervals of a perfect 5th on the I-IV-V-I chord progression

Chord Tuning

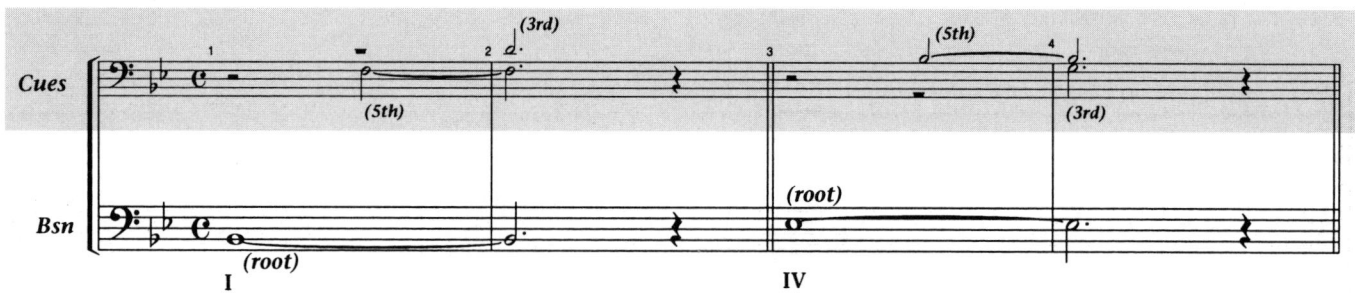

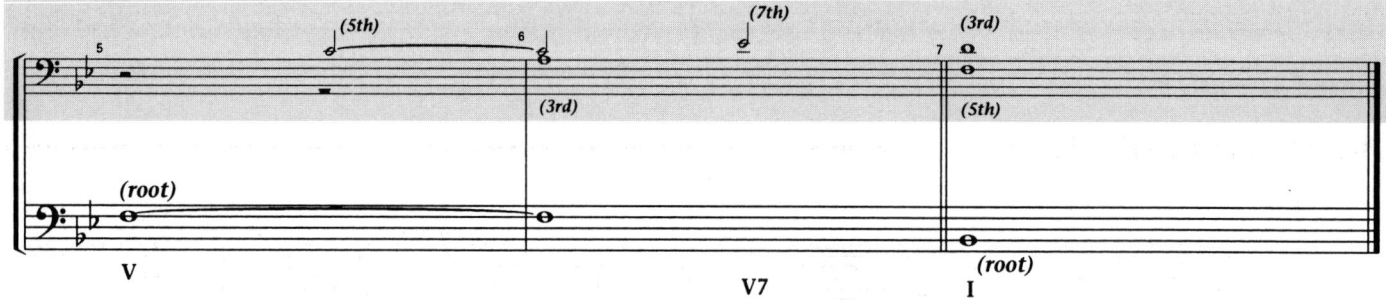

Chorale 1 (full band)

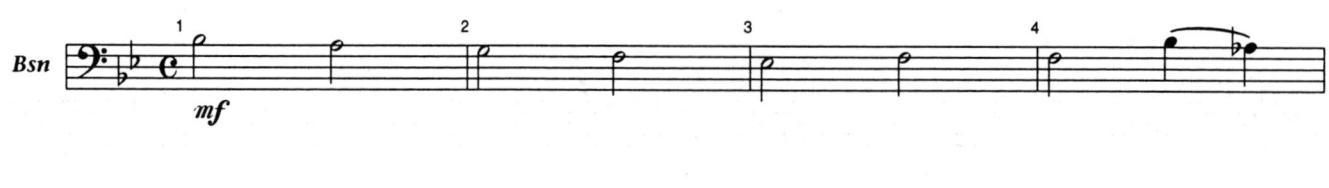

Chorale 2 (full band)

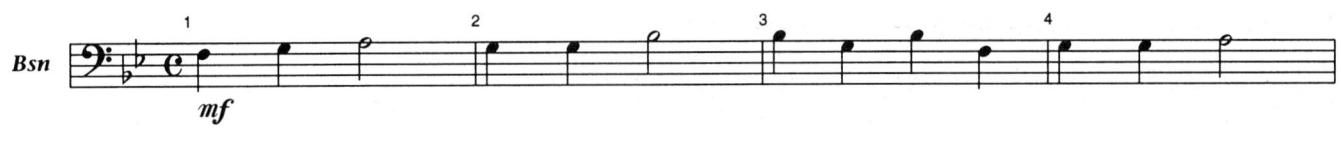

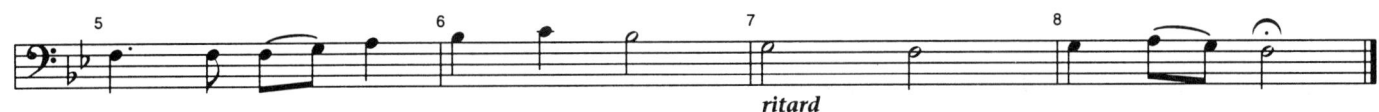

Chorale Melody on Chester

Chester Chorale (full band)

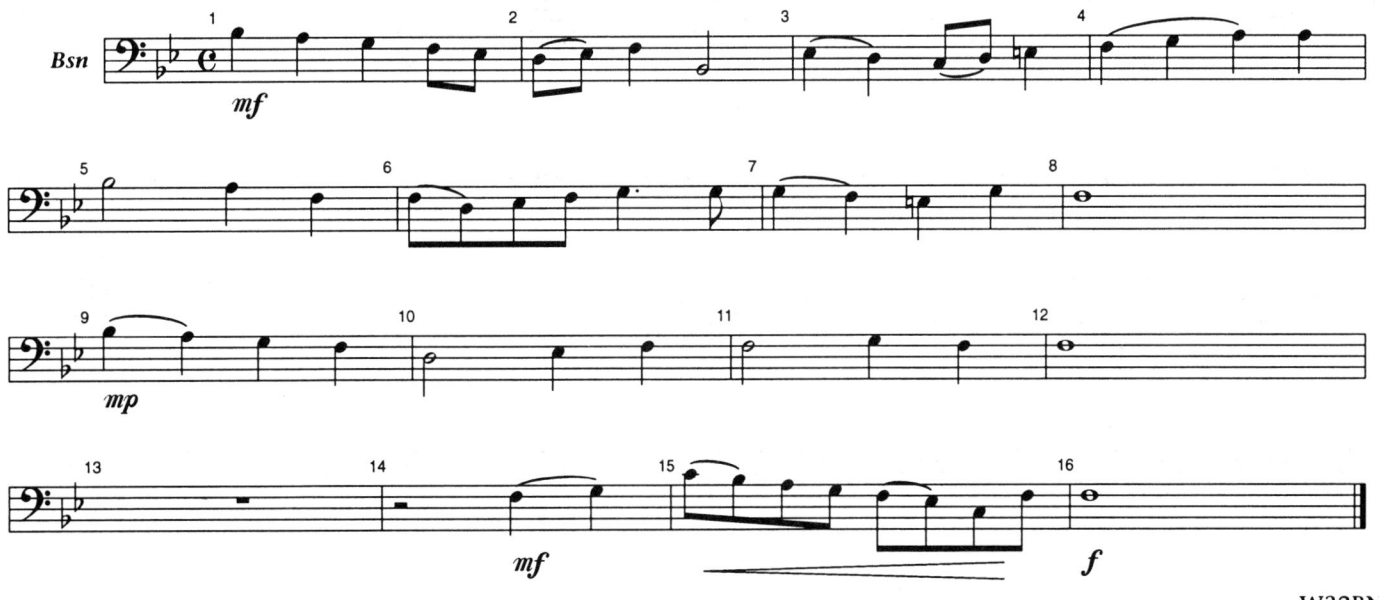

Chorales & Tuning Exercises in F

Interval Tuning

1 Intervals from tonic (major 3rd, perfect 4th, perfect 5th)

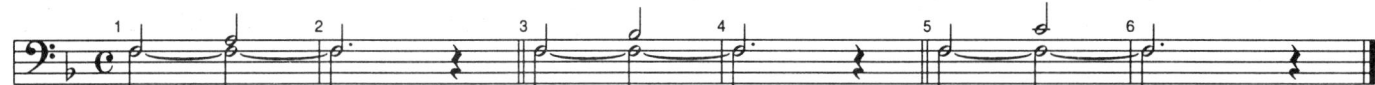

2 Intervals of a major 3rd on the I-IV-V-I chord progression

3 Intervals of a perfect 5th on the I-IV-V-I chord progression

Chord Tuning

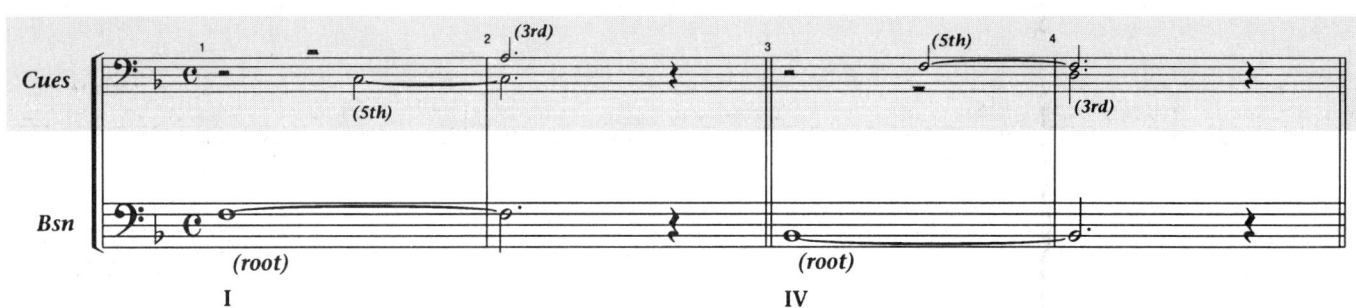

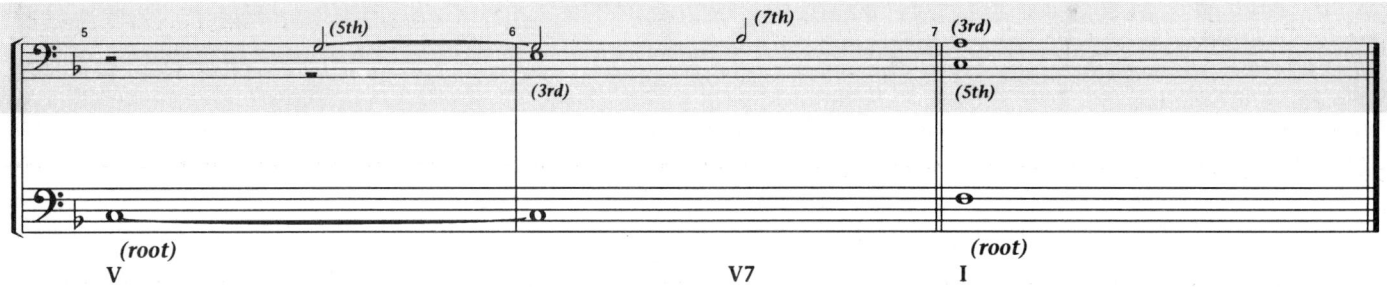

Chorale 3 (full band)

Chorale 4 (full band)

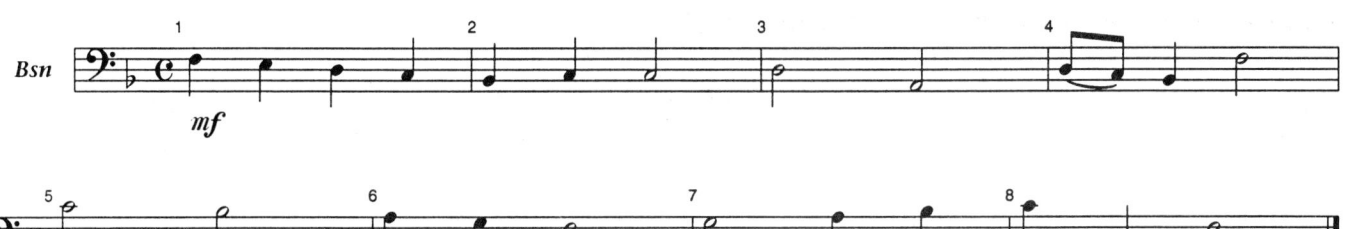

Chorale Melody on Bach 95

Bach 95 (full band)

Chorales & Tuning Exercises in E♭

Interval Tuning

1 Intervals from tonic (major 3rd, perfect 4th, perfect 5th)

2 Intervals of a major 3rd on the I-IV-V-I chord progression

3 Intervals of a perfect 5th on the I-IV-V-I chord progression

Chord Tuning

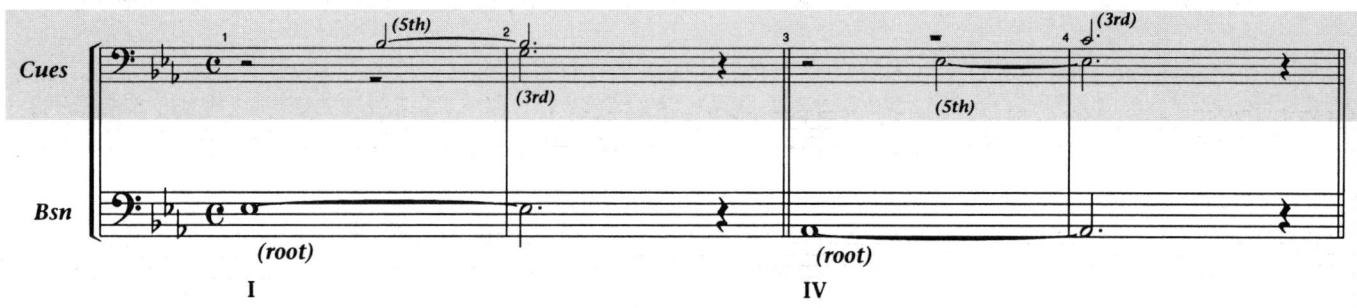

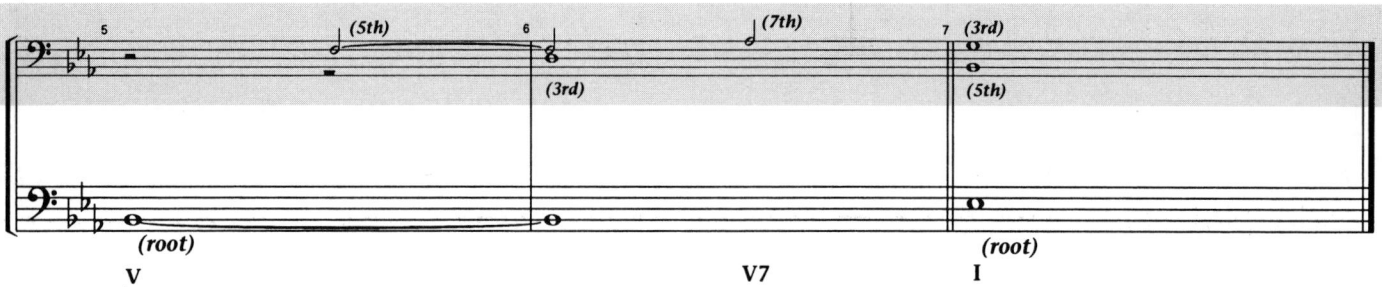

Chorale 5 (full band)

Chorale 6 (full band)

Chorale Melody on America

America (full band)

Chorale & Tuning Exercises in C

Interval Tuning

1 Intervals from tonic (major 3rd, perfect 4th, perfect 5th)

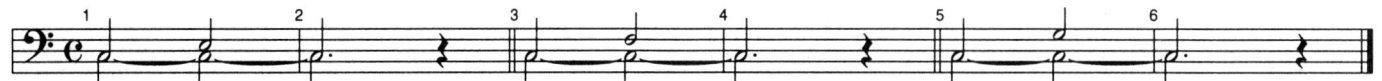

Chord Tuning

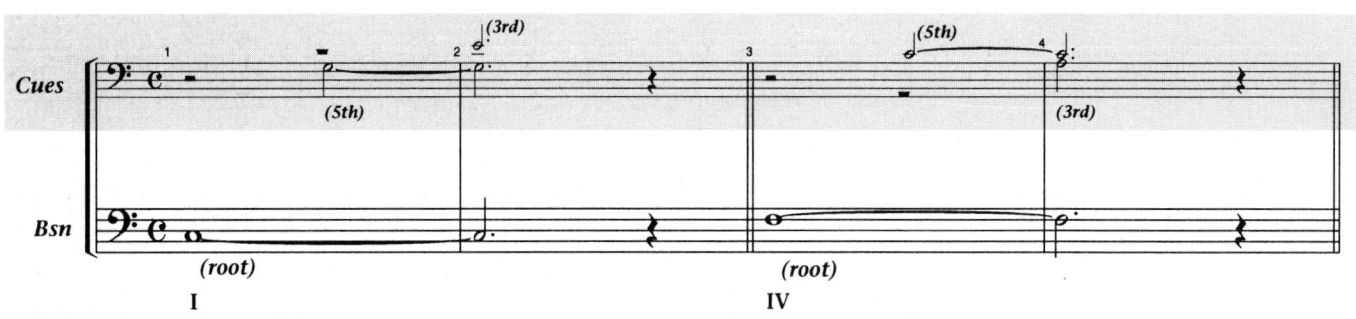

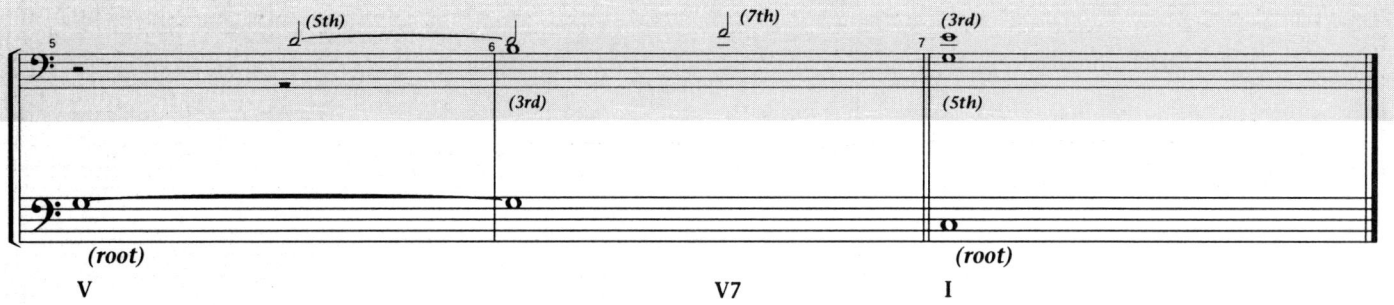

Air (full band)

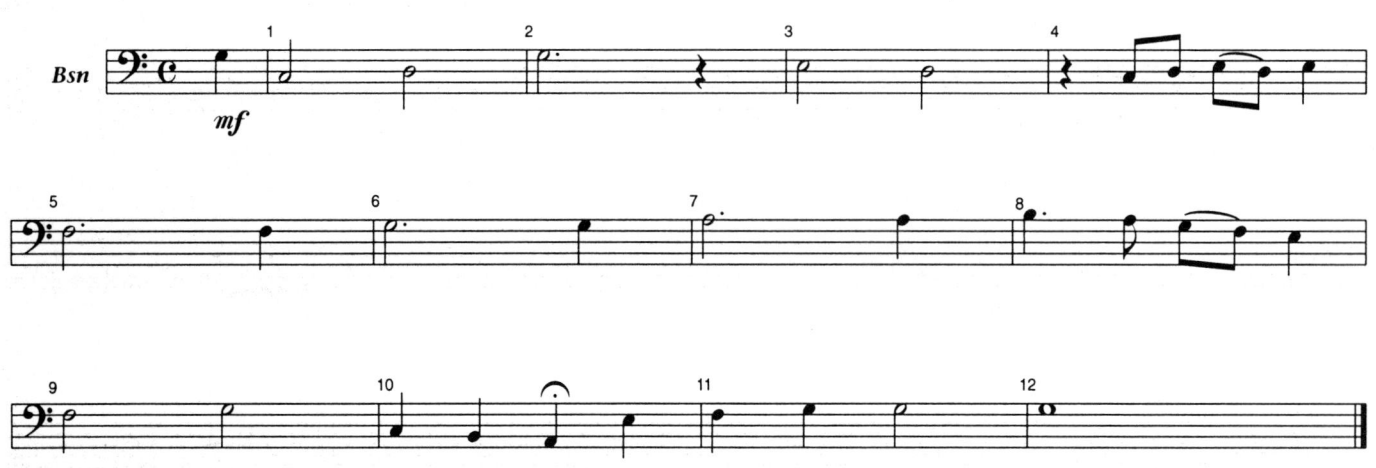

Chorale & Tuning Exercises in c minor

Interval Tuning

1 Intervals from tonic (minor 3rd, perfect 4th, perfect 5th)

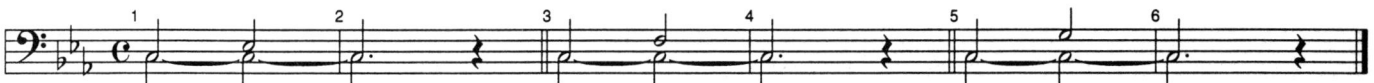

Chord Tuning

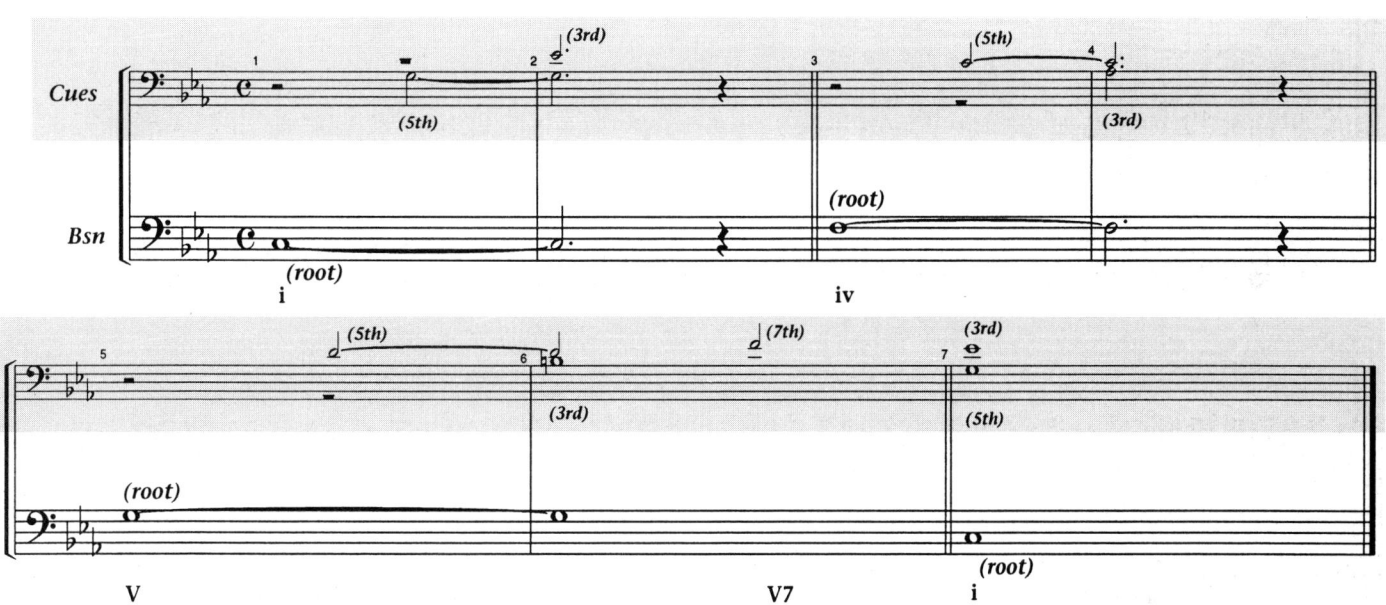

Greensleeves (full band)

Chorale & Tuning Exercises in G

Interval Tuning

1 Intervals from tonic (major 3rd, perfect 4th, perfect 5th)

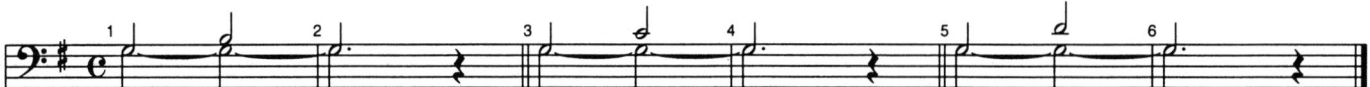

Chord Tuning

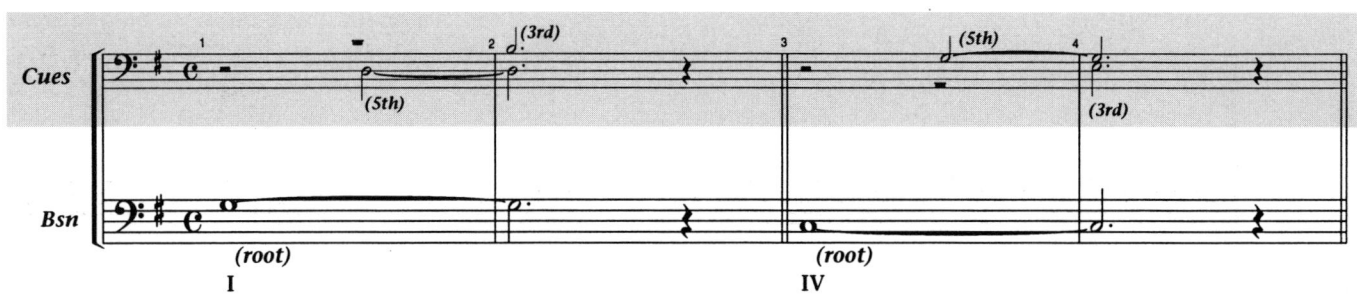

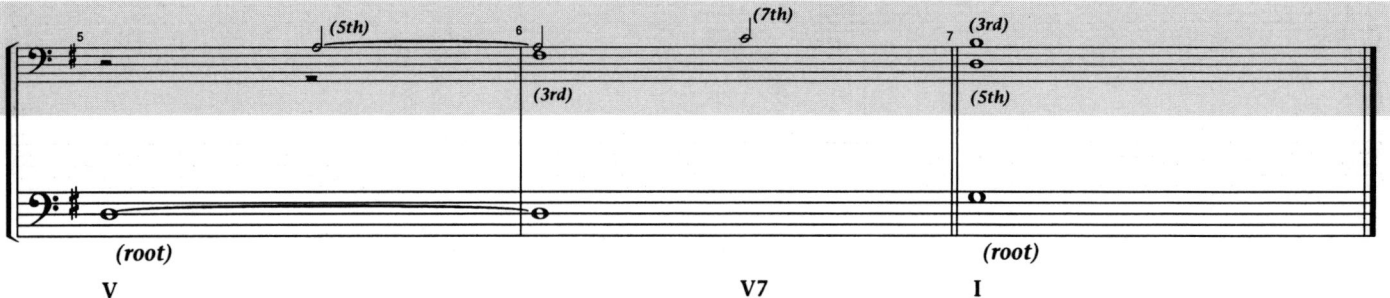

Pavane (full band)

Chorale & Tuning Exercises in g minor

Interval Tuning

1 Intervals from tonic (minor 3rd, perfect 4th, perfect 5th)

Chord Tuning

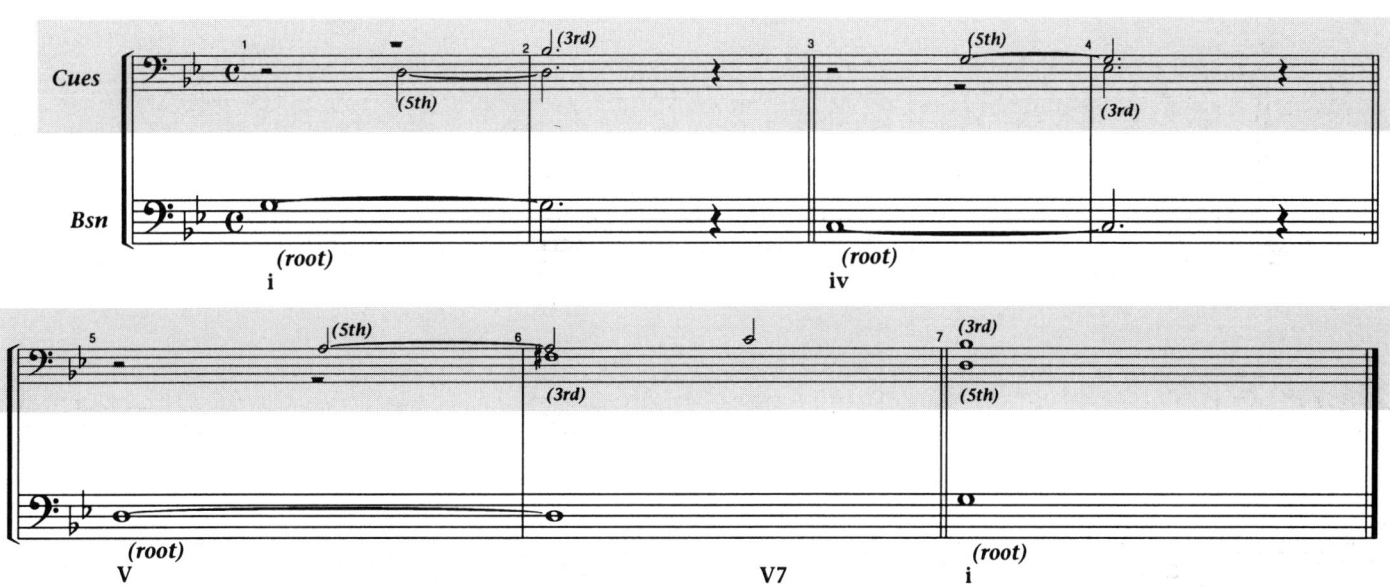

The Queene's Alman (full band)

Chorale & Tuning Exercises in A♭

Interval Tuning

1 Intervals from tonic (major 3rd, perfect 4th, perfect 5th)

Chord Tuning

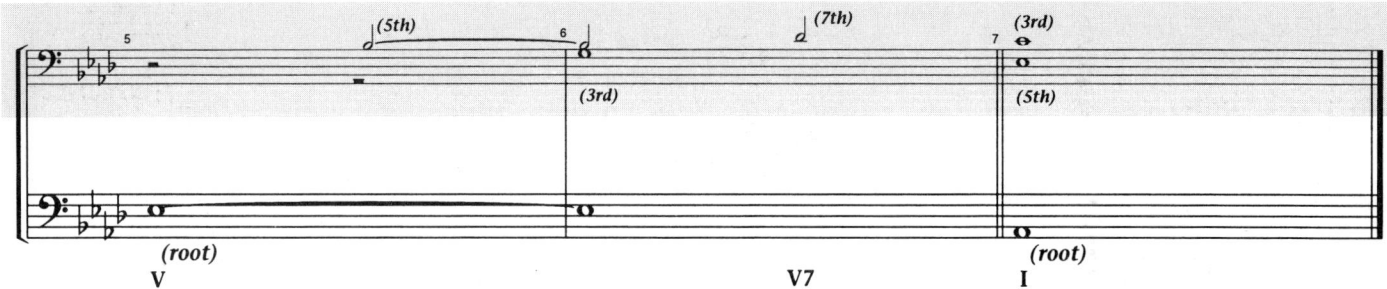

All Through the Night (full band)

Appendix

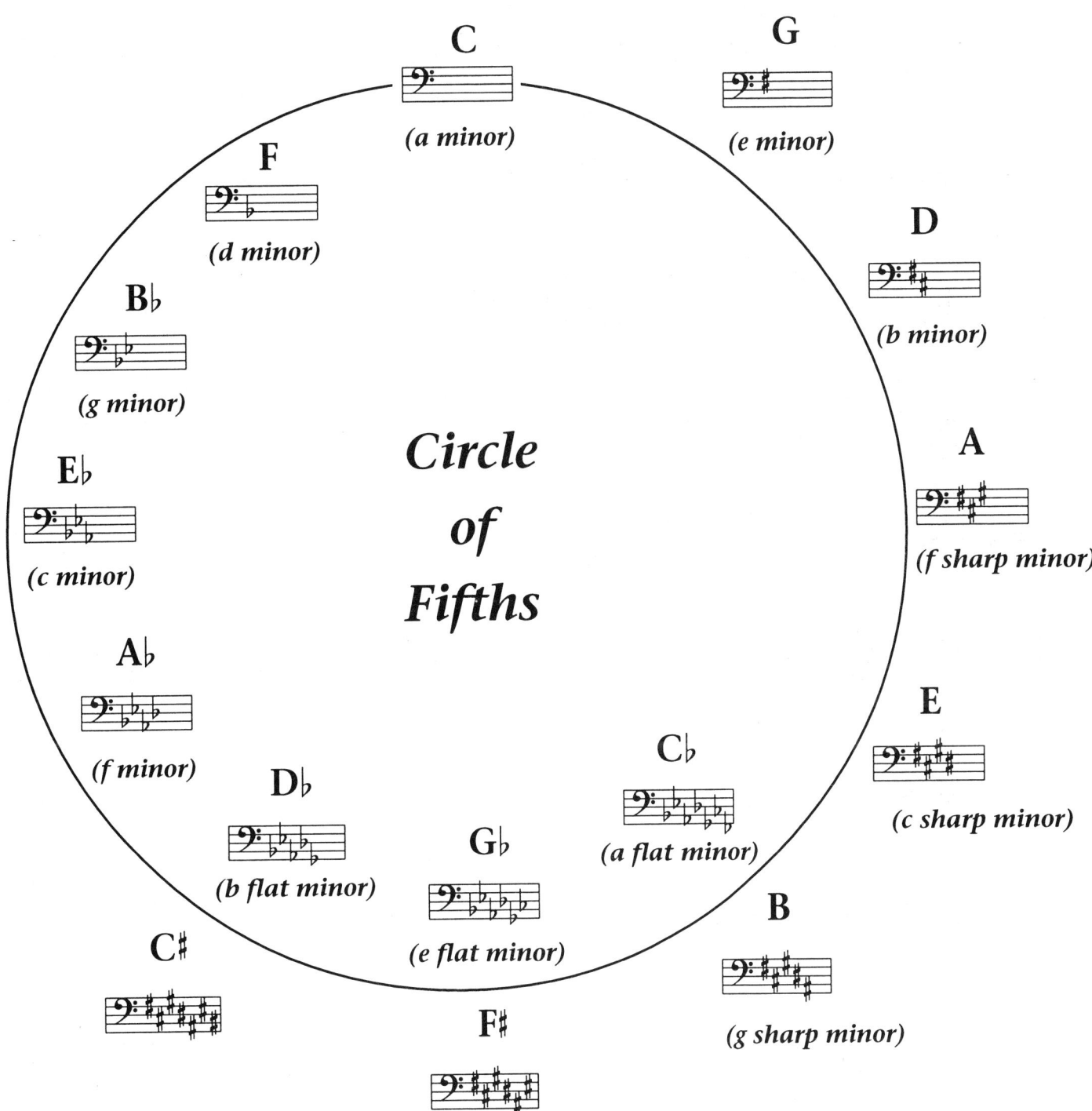

Circle of Fifths

One Octave Scales & Arpeggios

In All Twelve Major Key Signatures

Chromatic Exercises

B♭ Chromatic Scale

F Chromatic Scale

Full Range Scales

In All Twelve Major Key Signatures

Full Range Chromatic - Bassoons Only

Chromatic Scales

Bb

(also practice 8va)

B

(also practice 8va)

C

(also practice 8va)

Db

D

Eb

Major Arpeggios & Inversions

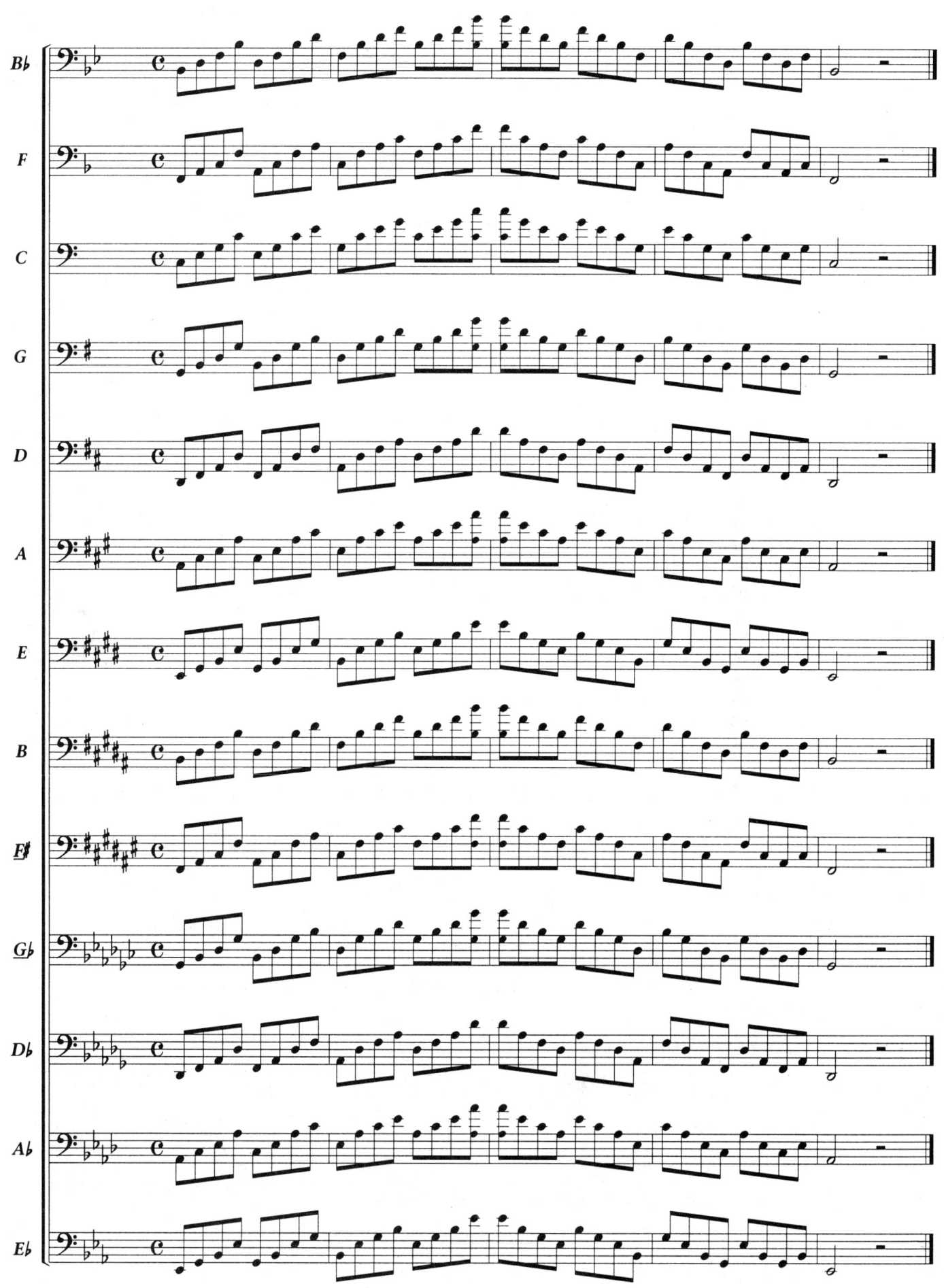